Goldi's first flute songbook

This book belongs to:

____

Goldi's First Flute Songbook

Copyright © 2024 by Stéphanie Superle

To request permission, contact the publisher at letsplay@fluteplay.ca

Library and Archives Canada Cataloguing in Publication
ISBN 978-1-7381189-5-3 (book)
ISBN 978-1-7381189-6-0 (paperback)
ISBN 978-1-7381189-7-7 (digital)

First edition

Goldi illustrations and cover art by Emily Johnston of Artio Design Co.
Fonts and graphics © Canva

Published by FlutePlay Printing Press
Families and educators, for more flute fun, visit us at fluteplay.ca

Table of Contents

Welcome to Goldi's First Flute Songbook! My name is Stéphanie Superle and I am a flutist, flute teacher, and the author of Goldi's First Flute Sounds! I'm thankful and excited you're here!

This songbook is intended to teach you all the fun and sparkly flute sounds you can make on your headjoint: Long and Short, High and Low, Wavy, and Whirly-twirly Roller Coaster sounds! If you've already read Goldi's First Flute Sounds, you know that sometimes making a sound on the headjoint can be tricky. I encourage you to follow Goldi and Zuzu to figure out how to consistently get a sparkly sound every day you play. If in doubt, ask an adult for help.

Once you're feeling confident making a sparkling flute sound on your headjoint, you're ready to play the music in this book! In Goldi's First Flute Songbook, I composed with pictures (graphic notation) rather than music notes (standard notation) so anyone can play - no prior musical experience required! Have fun following the shapes and sizes of the pictures to create your own unique interpretation of each song.

If you'd like to share your sparkly flute songs, don't be a stranger! You can tag me on social media or send me an email at the links below.

Happy music-making!

 @flute.play

 letsplay@fluteplay.ca

 @fluteplayfun

Long & Short

Long & Short Sounds

The songs in this section are played with our headjoint "**open**". This means we hold the headjoint with our left hand on the crown and our right hand supporting the end of the headjoint. Check out how Goldi holds her headjoint as an example:

Playing with your headjoint **open** also creates a "**high**" sound! We will explore high and low in the next section of this book so it's important to focus your time and attention in this section playing long & short sounds. Remember, you can always come back and play this section again with all low sounds after learning how to play high and low sounds in the next section!

Important Note: Because this music is composed using pictures (also known in music as graphic notation), every performance will be different! Have fun following the pictures to create your own unique interpretation every time you play!

Long Measures

One of the best ways to create a sparkly flute sound is to play long notes! Play each measuring tape as a long sound. Start on this page everyday you play and over time you'll be able to play even longer and sparklier notes on your headjoint!

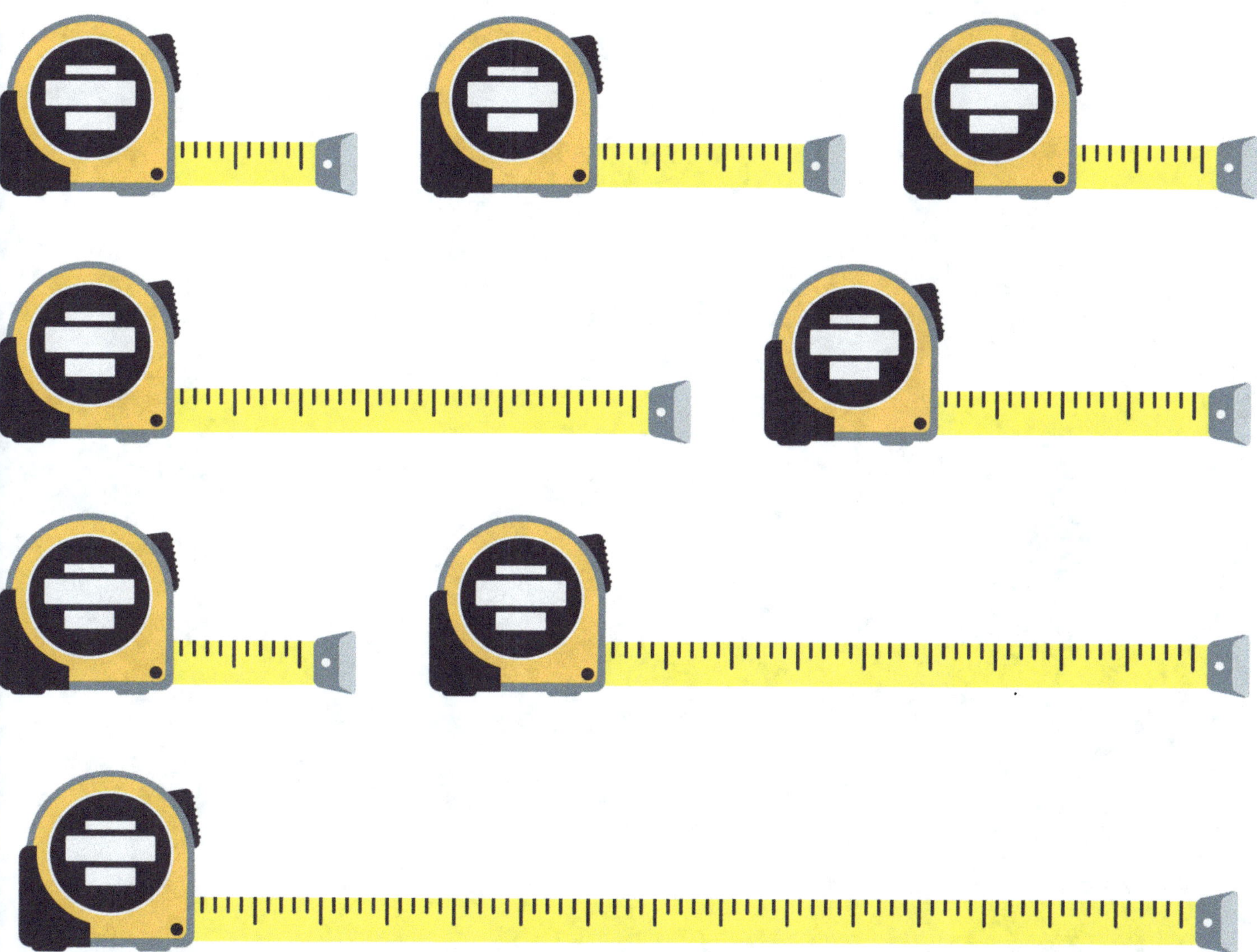

Snowflake Symphony

Moving across the picture from left to right, play the snowflakes you see as short notes on your headjoint. Look out for the snowstorm in the middle!

Pickle Juice

Peter Piper picked a peck of pickled peppers...in this song, play each pickle jar as a long note and the sliced pickles as short notes. Start every note with a "p" sound.

Flute Detectives

Help Goldi and Zuzu solve the flute mystery: Play short sounds when you see footprints and long sounds when you see a magnifying glass. Start every note with a "d" sound. Choose your own adventure every time you play this song!

Create your own!

After experimenting with long and short sounds, it's your turn to compose a tune with your unique mix. What will you create to showcase your new flute-tastic skills?

High & Low

High & Low Sounds

The songs in this section are played with our headjoint **open, closed,** and in the song "The Rainbow Slide" there are a few easy **slides!** This means you will continue to hold the headjoint with your left hand on the crown and your right hand will now move to create the high and low sounds. Here's a breakdown of each sound and it's hand movement:

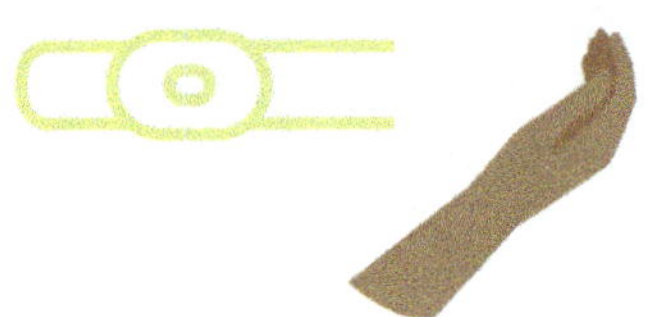

High sounds
- the end of the headjoint is "open"
- your right hand is away from the end of the headjoint or supporting the headjoint

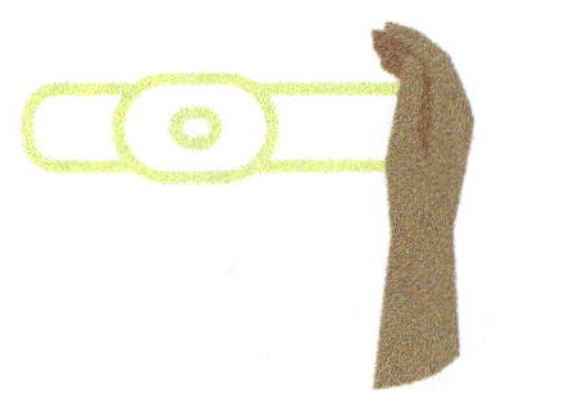

Low sounds
- the end of the headjoint is "closed"
- your right hand presses against the end of the headjoint creating a seal

High to Low sounds
- the headjoint starts open and ends closed
- your right hand index finger starts outside the headjoint and then slides in

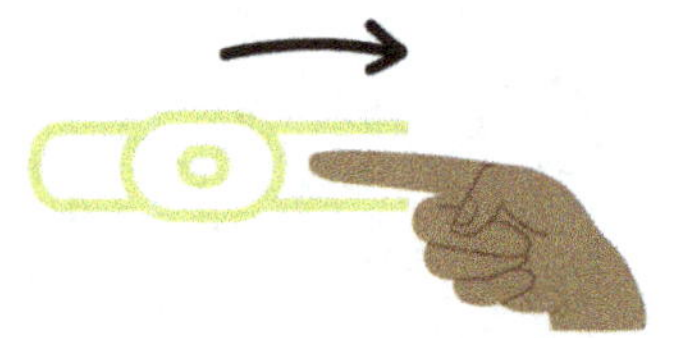

Low to High sounds
- the headjoint starts closed and ends open
- your right hand index finger starts inside the headjoint and then slides out

Prickly Pots

These prickly pots are perfect for exploring high and low sounds! When you see a tall cactus, play a high sound. When you see a short cactus, play a low sound. Try something new every time you play this song: for example, pots with two prickly plants can be played as two short notes! Remember to start every note with a "p".

Hot & Cold

Hot and cold, high and low! Tune into the thermometer's beat and let's make music with mercury! When it's scorching hot, play a high sound. When it's freezing cold, play a low sound. Start every note with a "t" sound.

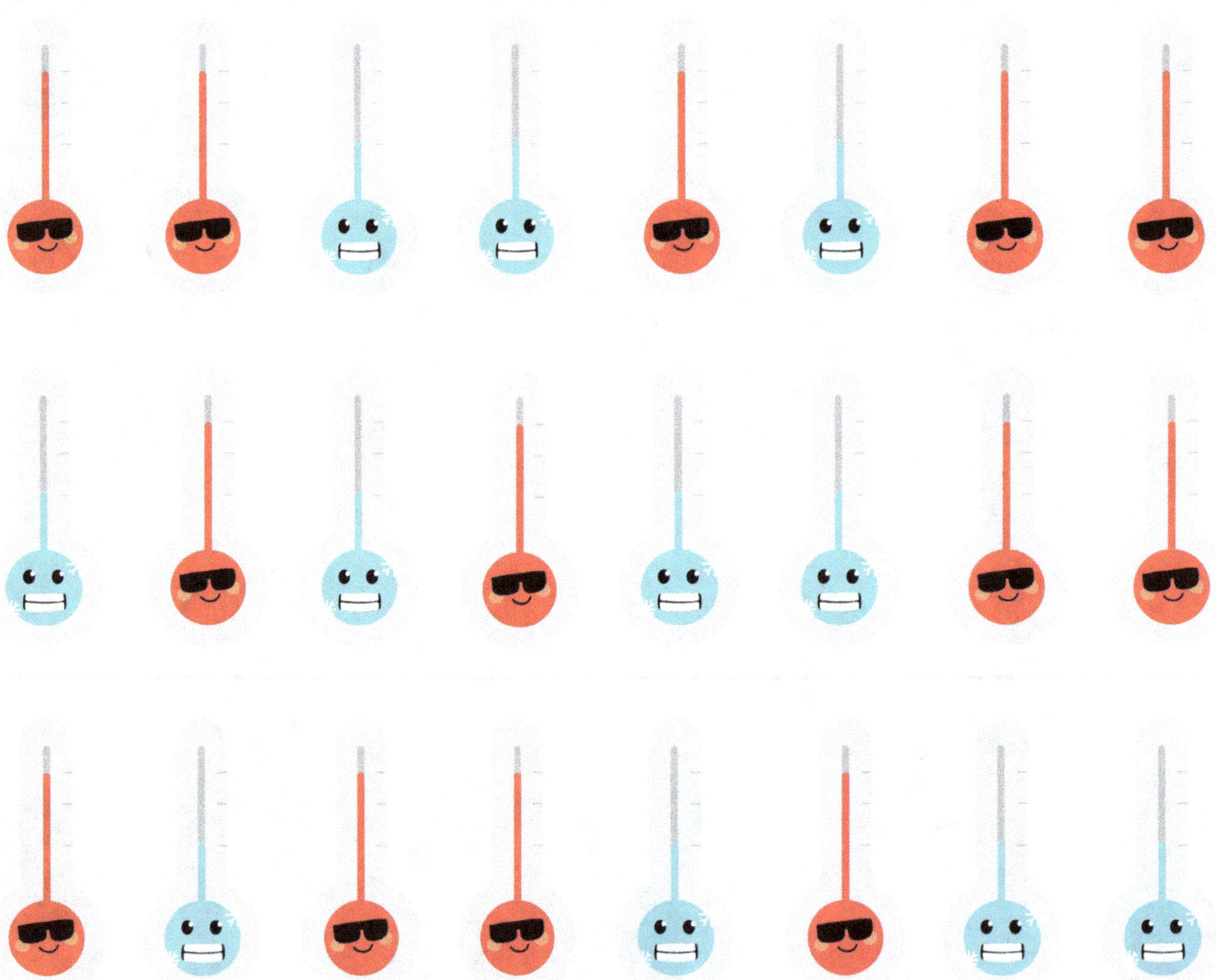

The Rainbow Slide

Welcome to the whimsical world of cloud hopping and rainbow slides. Imagine high clouds with your headjoint open and low clouds with your headjoint closed. And for those magical rainbow slides, let your right index finger dance in and out of the headjoint following the rainbow's shape!

With a Cherry on Top

Get ready to jam out on a delicious tune that mixes up all your flute skills: think long and short sounds AND high and low sounds! Keep reading for the full scoop...

Here are the musical ingredients for this sweet symphony:

High Sound = 5 scoops | **Low sound** = single scoop

Long sound = regular cones | **Short sound** = two cherries on top

Extra-long low sound = ice cream sundaes in a bowl

Create your own!

After experimenting with high and low sounds, it's your turn to compose a tune with your unique mix. What will you create to showcase your new flute-tastic skills?

Wavy

Wavy Sounds

The songs in this section are played with right hand index finger **slides!** (big slides, little slides–you decide!) This means you will continue to hold the headjoint with your left hand on the crown and your right hand will now move to create wavy sounds. Here's a breakdown of each sound and it's hand movement:

In the songs "Ice Cream Dreams" and "Temperamental" the goal is to create 3 distinct sounds to create a wavy song: High, Middle, and Low. This means your right hand index finger will find 3 specific spots with the headjoint to create a sound. Because every person is different, this finger placement will be different for everyone. Play around until you find the best place for your finger for each sound.

Try this flute finger formula to start:

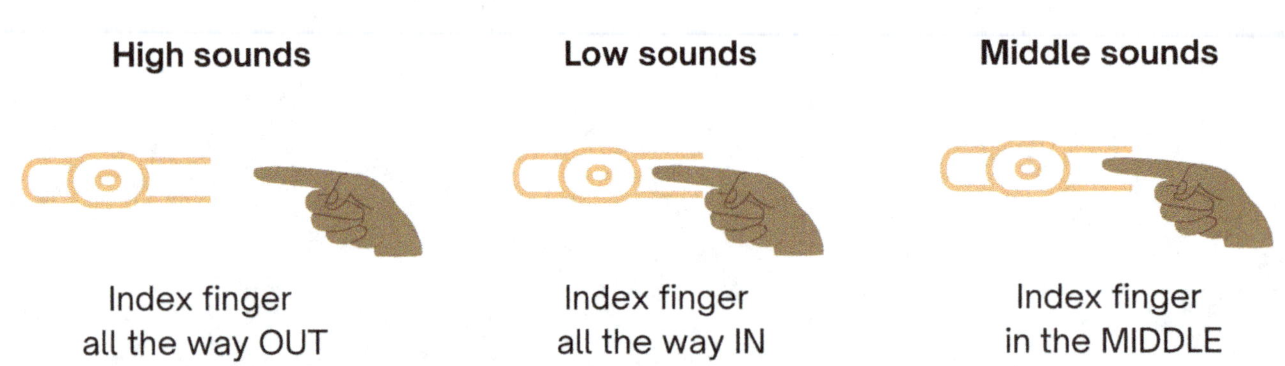

Flute Flight

Let's take to the skies for another musical adventure! Chase after the paper planes by copying their aerial acrobatics with your right index finger. You're the master of the skies so you determine the duration of each flight!

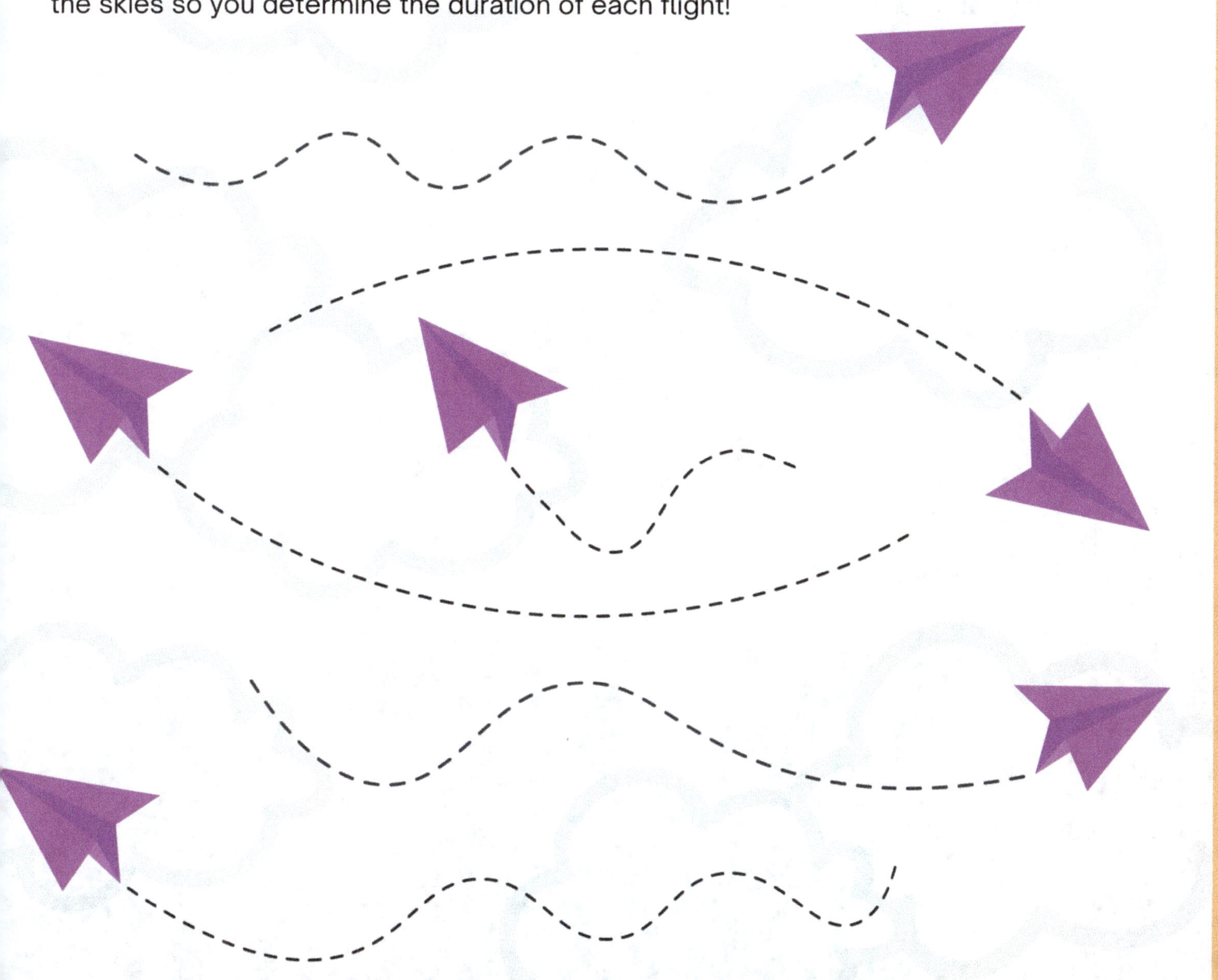

Playful Pencils

How many wavy shapes can you spot on this page? From orderly pencils to eccentric squiggles, there are many wavy shapes to play! And if you run out of ways to play what's here, you can always add your own wavy lines to the page.

Noodling Around

Feeling saucy? This next song might look im*pasta*ble but *ramen* calm and get ready to show off your wavy flute skills following the noodle shapes. Remember, the key to a great dish—and a great performance—is all in the sauce and the flair **you** bring. So grab your headjoint and let's make this a *pasta-tively* unforgettable performance!

Ice Cream Dreams

I scream, you scream, we all dream of ice cream... This song might ring a bell, but this time we're adding a twist! Imagine a swirly wave of ice cream: 5 scoops = high sounds, 3 scoops = middle sounds, and a single scoop = low sounds.

Temperamental

Too hot, too cold, or juuust right? By adding that middle sound, we're turning up the heat on these thermometers. Whether you start from the top or mix up the lines to shake things up, get ready to craft your own sizzling ending!

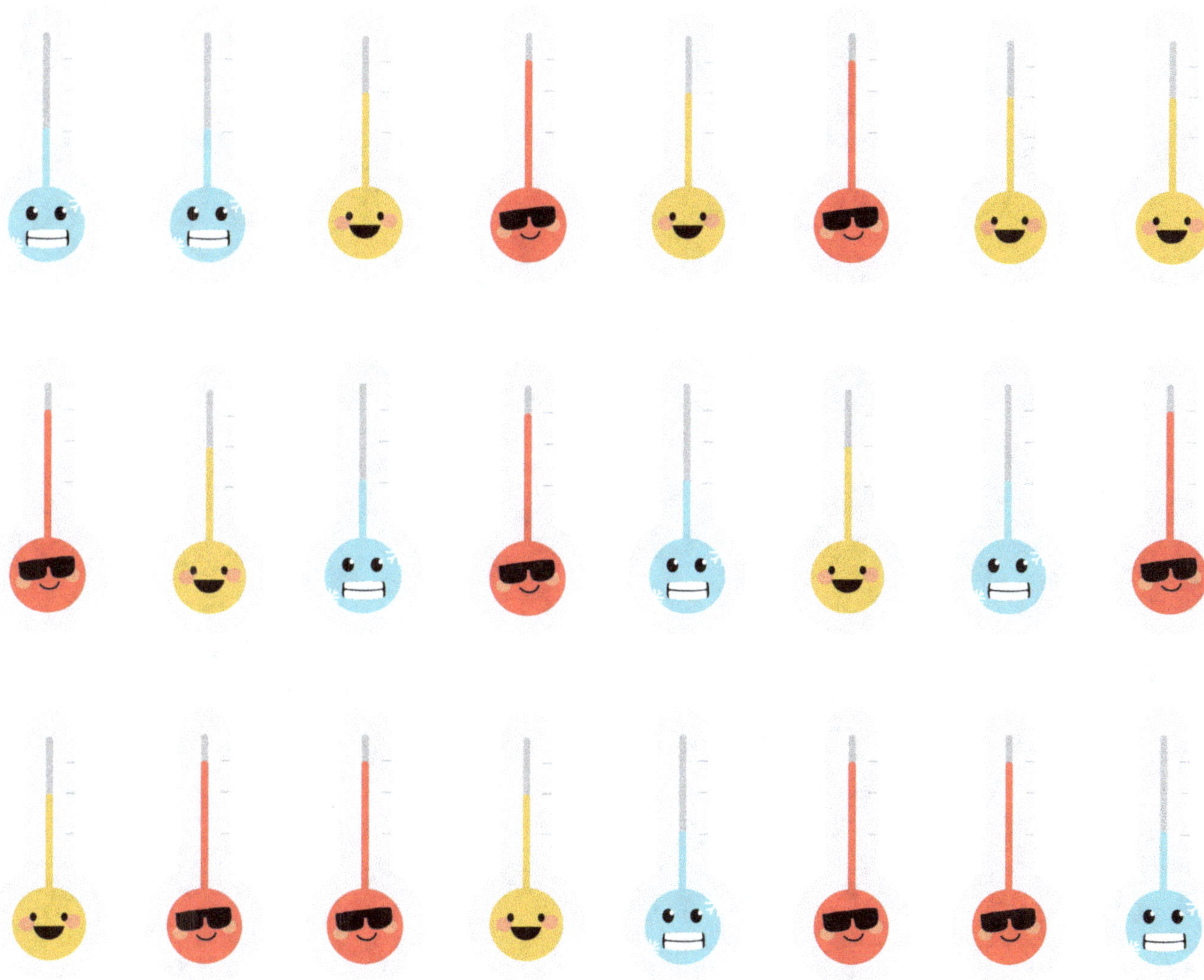

Create your own!

After experimenting with wavy sounds, it's your turn to compose a tune with your unique mix. What will you create to showcase your new flute-tastic skills?

Whirly-twirly

Roller Coaster

Whirly-twirly Roller Coaster Sounds

The songs in this section are played with right hand index finger **whirly-twirly slides!** This means you will continue to hold the headjoint with your left hand on the crown and your right hand will now slide and wiggle and/or twirl to create whirly-twirly roller coaster sounds. Here's a breakdown of each sound and it's hand movement:

High to Low sounds

Low to High sounds

For each song, follow the shapes of the pictures for a whirly-twirly combination of high, low, middle, and everything in between! The final 2 songs, "Shooting Stars" and "Flute Fantasy", showcase every kind of sound you've learned in this book! Have fun showing off your flute skills by creating unique performances every time you play!

Whether you're playing for an audience or just for yourself, remember that music is an expression of your creativity. Embrace the joy of each note, and let your passion for the flute shine through every performance. Don't be afraid to experiment with dynamics (soft & loud), tempo (fast & slow), and articulation (long & short) to bring each piece to life in your own special way. Happy music-making, and may your flute journey be filled with inspiration and delight!

Whirly-twirly Warm-up

Whirly-twirly sounds require your right hand and right hand index finger to be loose and relaxed so it can move freely in and out of the headjoint. Let's warm-up by following the movement of this bright kaleidoscope of colours! Play one colour in a single breath, then play a few colours in a row for a longer sound.

Rainbow Ribbons

Follow the swirls and twirls of these vibrant ribbons by sliding your right index finger in and out of your headjoint. Once you've mastered each ribbon's tune, flip it upside down for an extra twist!

Roller Coaster Ride

This roller coaster welcomes all thrill-seekers, so hop on board! Each car promises a distinct experience, filled with surprises at every twist and turn. Get ready, fasten your seatbelt, and enjoy selecting a new coaster car each time you play this tune for a new whirly-twirly adventure!

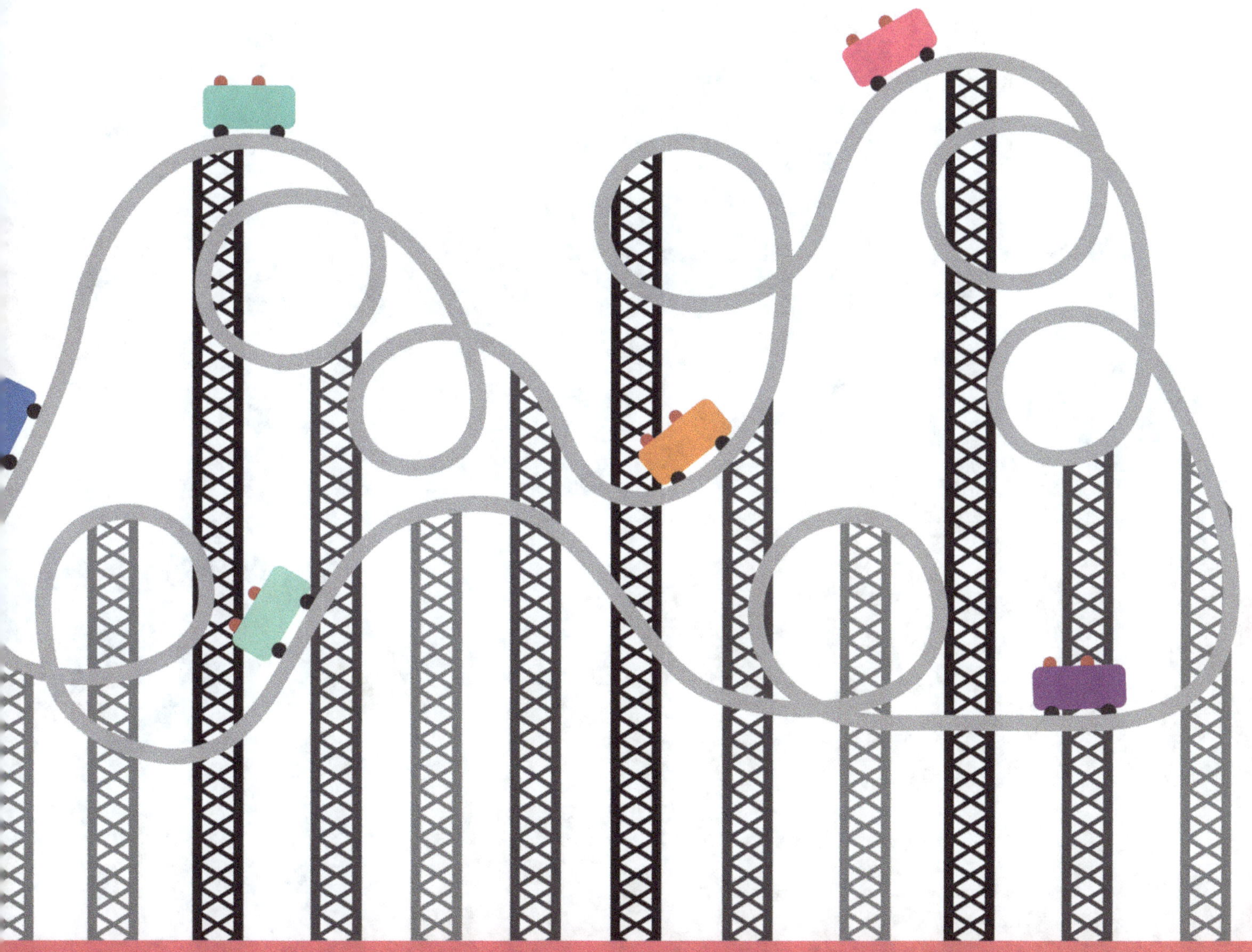

Shooting Stars

We're taking our flute game to galactic levels! Here is your chance to flaunt all the flute sounds you've mastered. Pick a new alien friend each time you perform this tune for an interstellar jam session that's truly out of this world!

Flute Fantasy

Welcome to the flute-tastic finale of our flute adventure! Step into a whimsical world where your flute skills shine and your sparkly sounds take flight! What magical tune will you dream up in this musical wonderland?

Create your own!

After experimenting with whirly-twirly roller coaster sounds, it's your turn to compose a tune with your unique mix. What will you create to showcase your new flute-tastic skills?

CERTIFICATE
Congratulations to
for challenging yourself, for trying new things, and for completing all the songs in Goldi's First Flute Songbook!
Signed
Date